I0818525

CITY CRITTERS
Foxes
by Clare Koll
BLASTOFF! READERS
1
BELLWETHER MEDIA • MINNEAPOLIS, MN

Blastoff! Readers are carefully developed by literacy experts to build reading stamina and move students toward fluency by combining standards-based content with developmentally appropriate text.

LEVELS

Level 1 provides the most support through repetition of high-frequency words, light text, predictable sentence patterns, and strong visual support.

Level 2 offers early readers a bit more challenge through varied sentences, increased text load, and text-supportive special features.

Level 3 advances early-fluent readers toward fluency through increased text load, less reliance on photos, advancing concepts, longer sentences, and more complex special features.

★ **Blastoff! Universe**

Reading Level

Grade K

Grades 1–3

Grade 4

This edition first published in 2025 by Bellwether Media, Inc.

Library of Congress Cataloging-in-Publication Data

Names: Koll, Clare, author.
Title: Foxes / by Clare Koll.
Description: Minneapolis, MN : Bellwether Media, Inc., 2025. | Series: Blastoff! Readers: City Critters | Includes bibliographical references and index. | Audience: Ages 5-8 | Audience: Grades K-1 | Summary: "Developed by literacy experts for students in kindergarten through grade three, this book introduces foxes in cities to young readers through leveled text and related photos"– Provided by publisher.
Identifiers: LCCN 2024035382 (print) | LCCN 2024035383 (ebook) | ISBN 9798893042177 (library binding) | ISBN 9798893043143 (ebook)
Subjects: LCSH: Foxes–Juvenile literature. | Urban animals–Juvenile literature.
Classification: LCC QL737.C22 K765 2025 (print) | LCC QL737.C22 (ebook) | DDC 599.775–dc23/eng/20231108
LC record available at https://lccn.loc.gov/2024035382
LC ebook record available at https://lccn.loc.gov/2024035383

Editor: Christina Leaf Designer: Gabriel Hilger

Printed in the United States of America, North Mankato, MN.

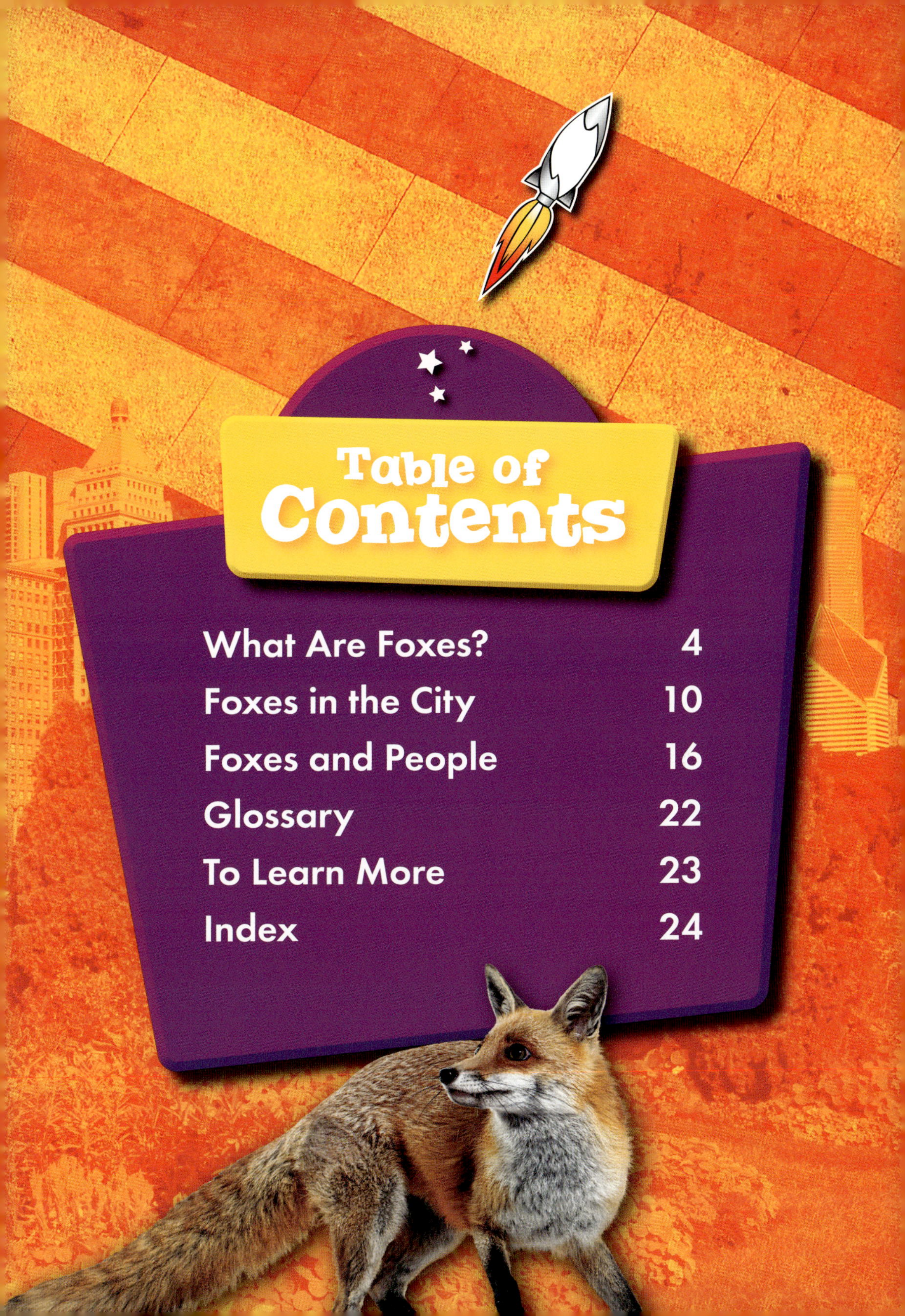

Table of Contents

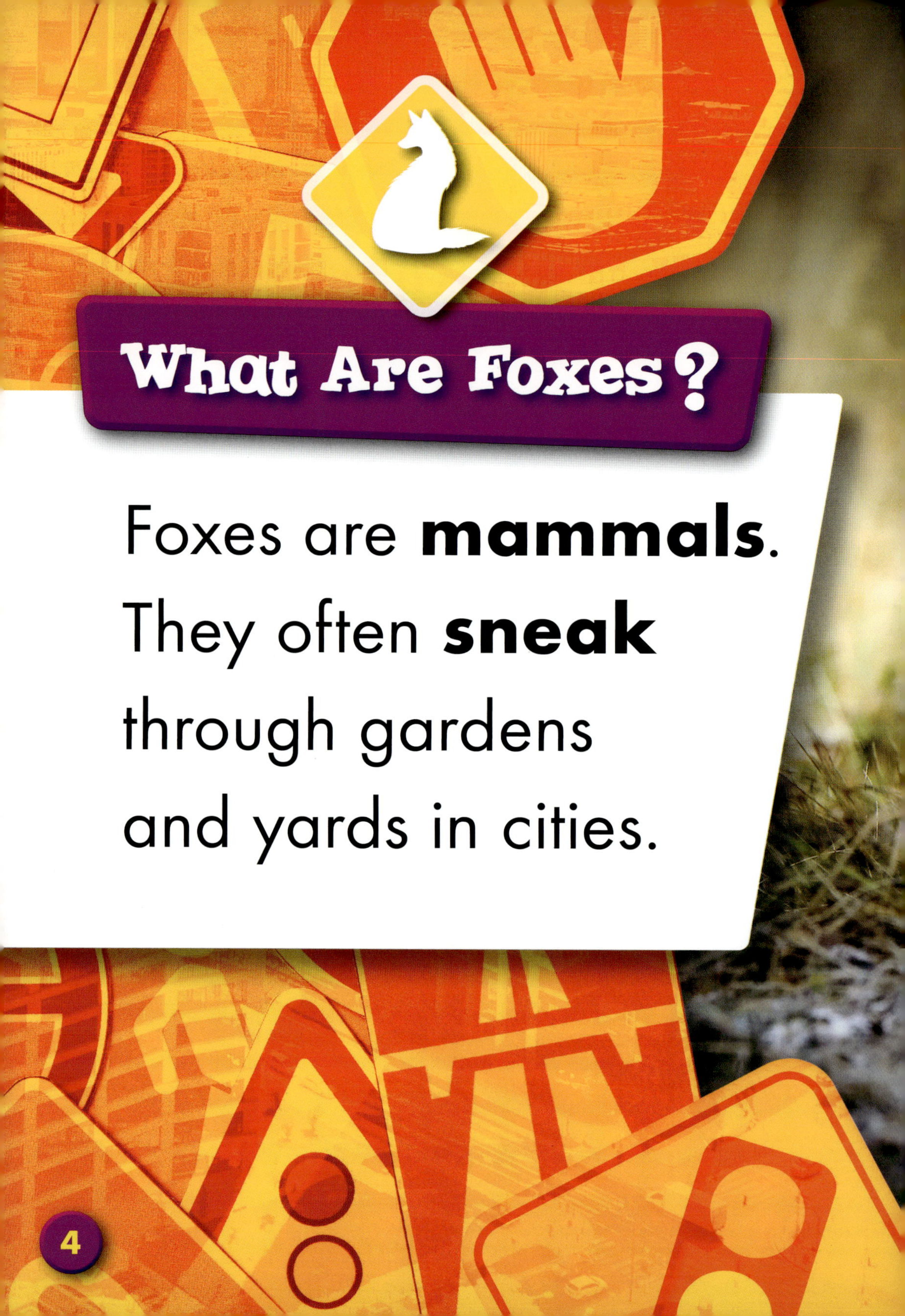

What Are Foxes?

Foxes are **mammals**. They often **sneak** through gardens and yards in cities.

Foxes have red, brown, or gray fur. Fluffy tails keep them warm in winter.

Common City Foxes
red fox
gray fox
tail

Pointed ears help foxes hear well. Long **snouts** help them smell food.

snout
ears

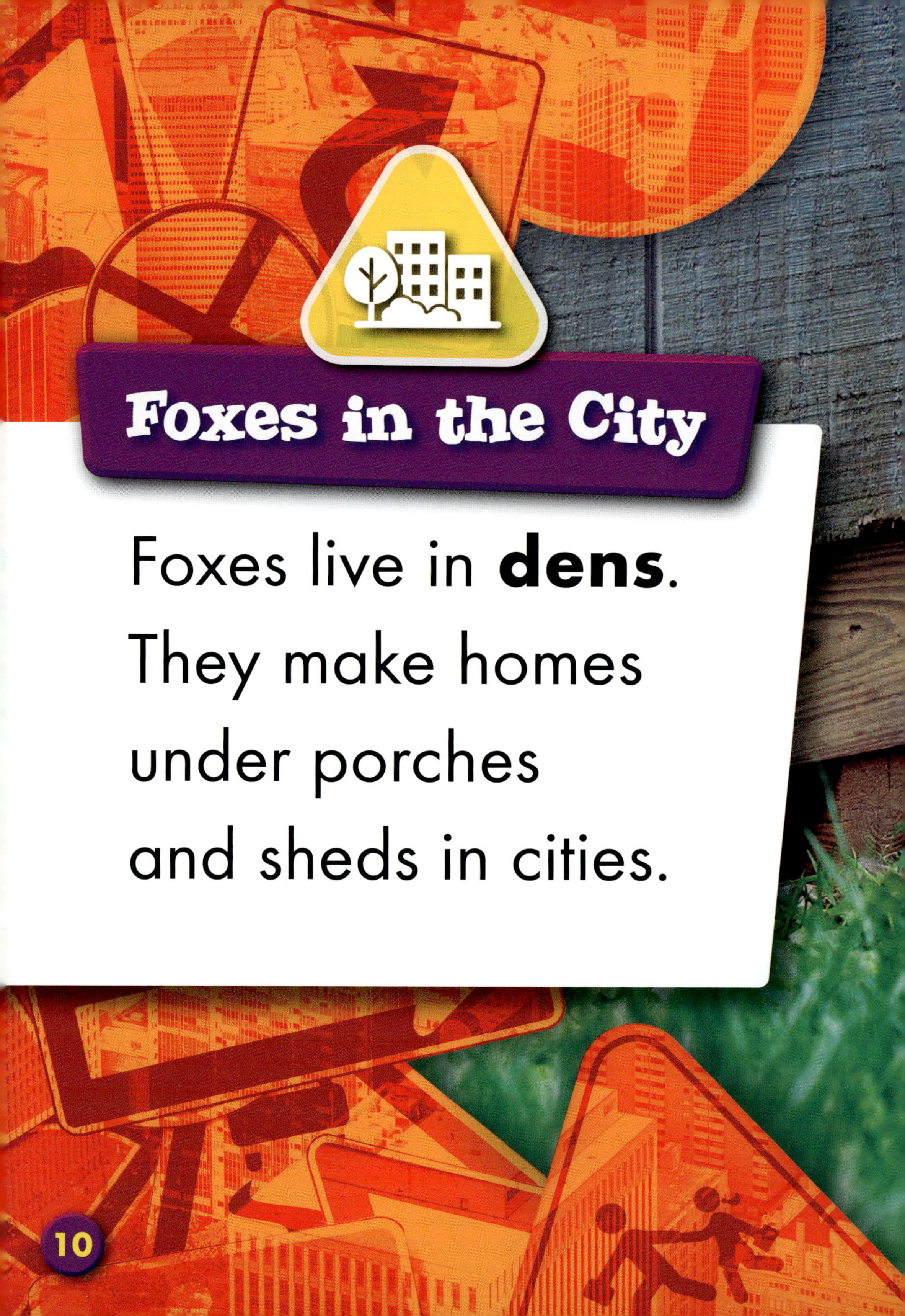

Foxes in the City

Foxes live in **dens**. They make homes under porches and sheds in cities.

den
Fox Homes
under porches
under sheds
under bushes

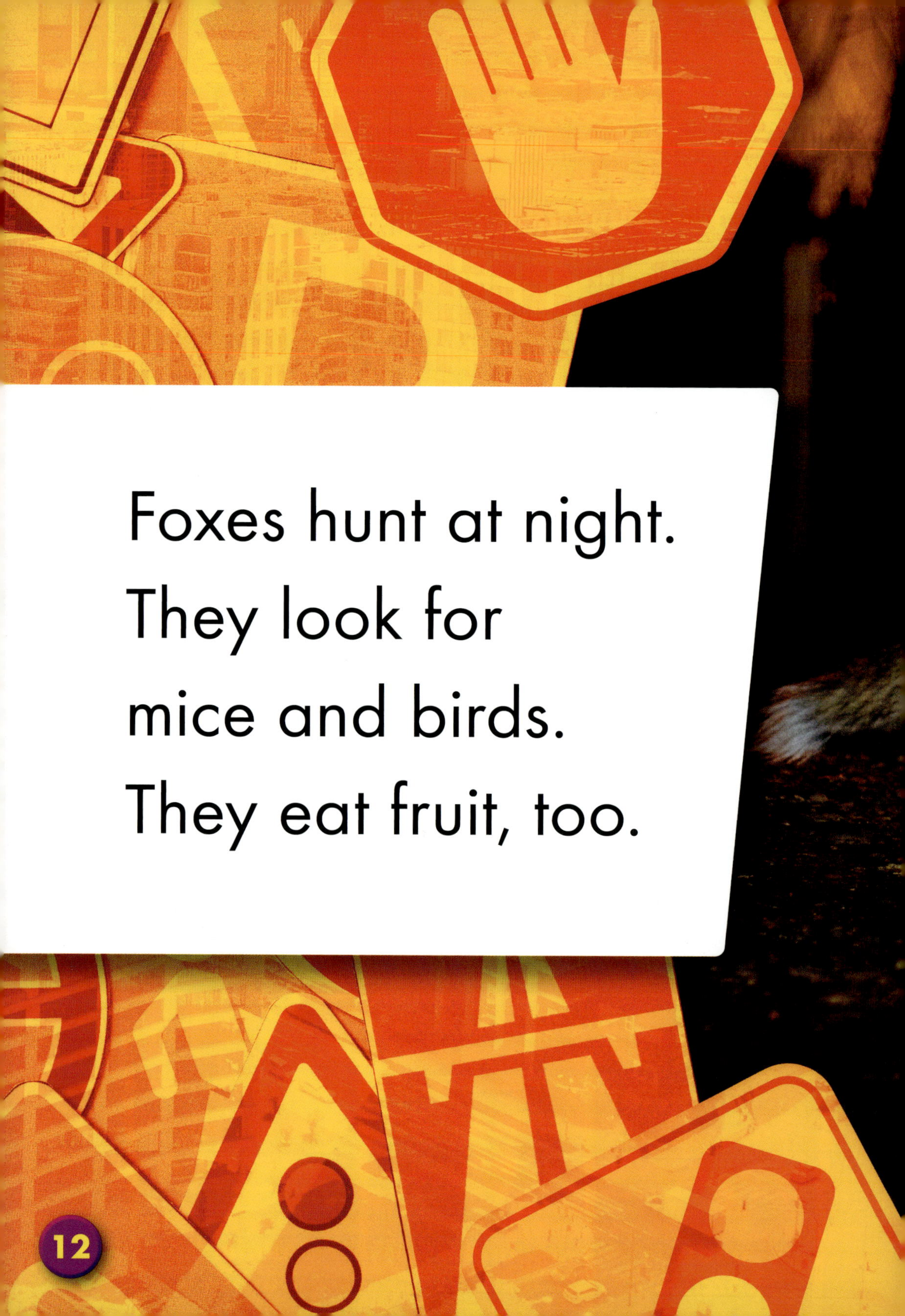

Foxes hunt at night.
They look for
mice and birds.
They eat fruit, too.

Fox Food
mice
fruit
people food

They eat people food. They store extra food in **caches**.

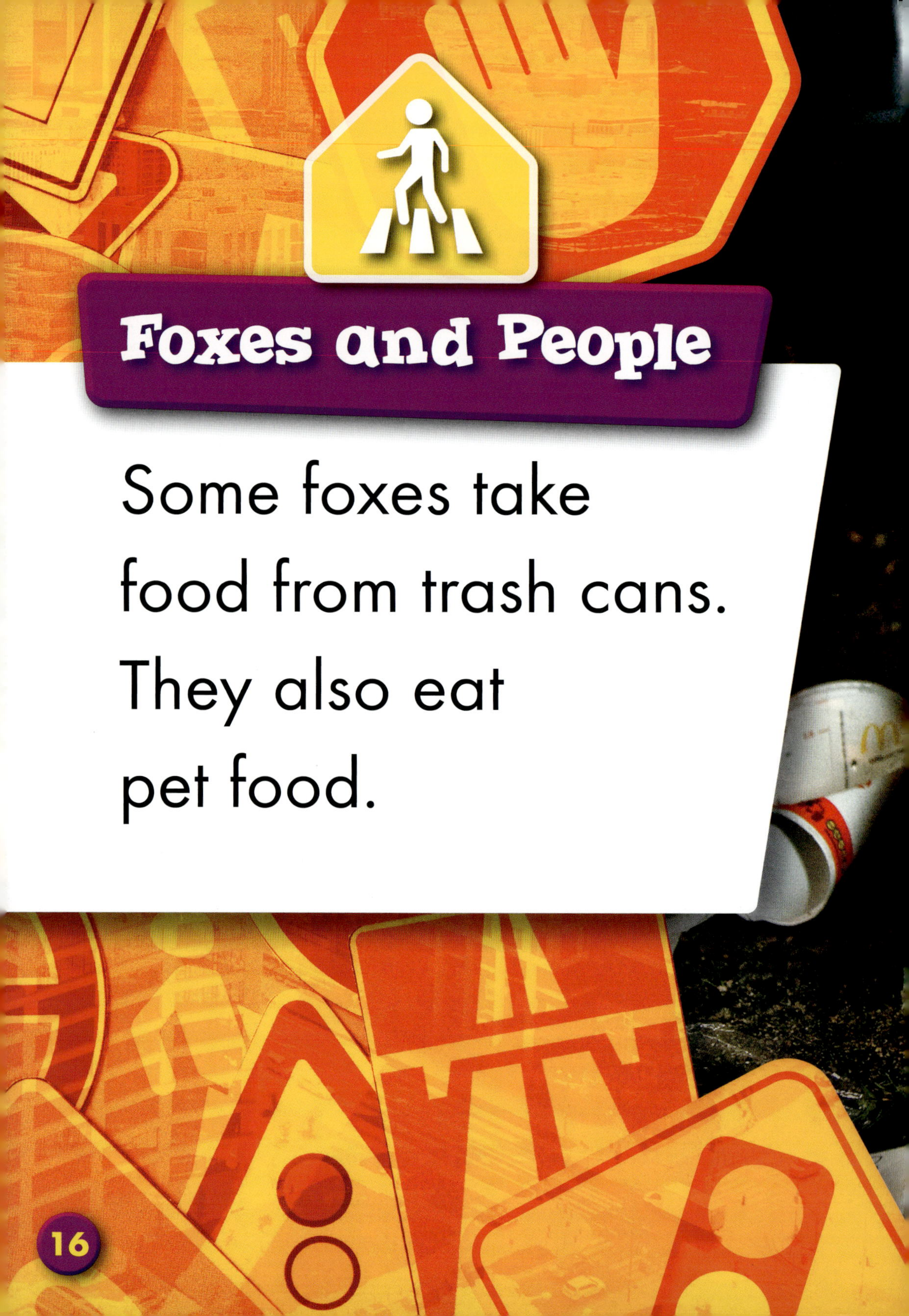

Foxes and People

Some foxes take food from trash cans. They also eat pet food.

Some people like to spot foxes. Others chase them away.

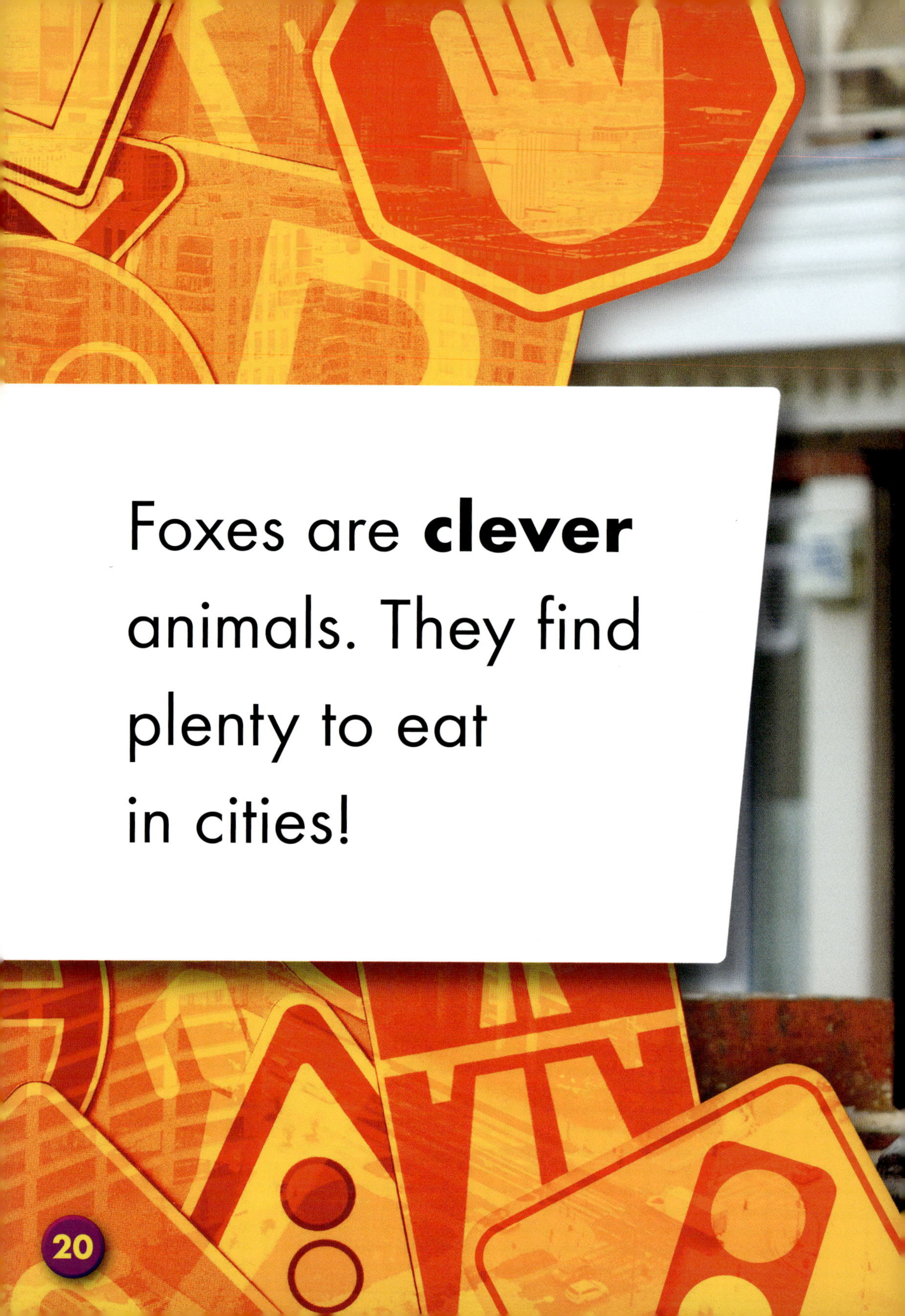

Foxes are **clever** animals. They find plenty to eat in cities!

Glossary

caches

hidden places used to store food

mammals

warm-blooded animals that have backbones and feed their young milk

clever

smart or quick to learn

sneak

to move in secret

dens

sheltered places

snouts

the noses and mouths of some animals

To Learn More

AT THE LIBRARY

Leaf, Christina. *Baby Foxes.* Minneapolis, Minn.: Bellwether Media, 2022.

McDonald, Amy. *Foxes.* Minneapolis, Minn.: Bellwether Media, 2021.

Perish, Patrick. *Red Foxes.* Minneapolis, Minn.: Bellwether Media, 2022.

ON THE WEB

FACTSURFER

Factsurfer.com gives you a safe, fun way to find more information.

1. Go to www.factsurfer.com.
2. Enter "foxes" into the search box and click 🔍.
3. Select your book cover to see a list of related content.

Index

The images in this book are reproduced through the courtesy of: valleyboi63, front cover (fox); Kubrak78, front cover (city); Eric Isselee, pp. 4, 7 (red fox); WildMedia, pp. 4-5; Paul Hartley, pp. 6-7; Travis Potter, p. 7 (gray fox); Rachel Bennett, pp. 8-9; Basia Seaman, pp. 10-11, 22 (dens); portsmouthnhcharley, p. 11 (under porches); ideeone, p. 11 (under sheds); Randall Vermillion, p. 11 (under bushes); Jamie_Hall, pp. 12-13; Ihor Hvozdetskyi, p. 13 (mice); Primi2, p. 13 (fruit); Zako, p. 13 (people food); Andyworks, pp. 14-15; Nature Picture Library/ Alamy Stock Photo, pp. 16-17; Vaclav Matous, pp. 18-19; Peter Crome/ Alamy Stock Photo, pp. 20-21; DZarzycka, p. 22 (caches); davidhills, p. 22 (clever); Robert Enriquez, p. 22 (mammals); tonytao, p. 22 (sneak); Lukas Gojda, p. 22 (snouts).